The Five Minute Guide to HTML 5.0

The New Fifth Core Element Architecture of the World Wide Web

Written by

Alastair R Agutter

The Five Minute Guide To HTML 5.0

COVER DESIGN:
By Alastair R Agutter

ORIGINAL DRAWINGS AND ILLUSTRATIONS
By Alastair R Agutter

PHOTOGRAPHS COURTESY OF
Alastair R Agutter and W3C

www.alastairagutter.com

PUBLISHED BY

Create Space Independent Publishing
An Amazon Group Company

First Edition Published: 23rd May 2014

ISBN-10: 1499661037

ISBN-13: 978-1499661033

Contents

Chapter Ten

About the Author and Related Publications

Introduction

Welcome to "The Five Minute Guide to HTML 5.0" a short book and guide to familiarize web site owners, developers, webmaster enthusiasts and web users to the World of HTML 5.0 the new fifth core element language architecture created by the World Wide Web Consortium.

A New Era for the World Wide Web the World of HTML 5.0

For two years now I have been developing HTML 5.0 and have found the journey positive in every way as a Senior WWW Developer regarding the new RDFa framework.

So what is HTML 5.0 and what is the difference?

Around 8 years ago, I wrote an academic paper with reference to concerns of the World Wide Web called "The Chaos Theory" and believed then, as I do today that the failure to create a more cohesive and structure framework of authoring for the web, with an ever increasing demand by more users and data could cause a genuine threat where the World Wide Web could result in being unable to function.

The new fifth core element architecture of HTML 5.0 addresses many of these concerns and the authoring of the new framework makes HTML again a friend to program rendering browser engines where web sites and pages can be delivered faster and more effectively from pure coding.

I have been encouraged by the changes and improvements for there have been many changes for creating a far more dynamic environment for a greater user experience.

So welcome to "The Five Minute Guide to HTML 5.0"

Alastair Agutter

Chapter One ≫

Web Semantics Giving Meaning to Structure

Giving meaning to structure with web semantics is at the front and centre with HTML 5.0.

Chapter One: An introduction to HTML 5.0 Web Semantics

New Html 5.0 framework provides richer sets of tags, along with RDFa, micro data, and micro formats and all are enabling a more useful, data driven web for both programmers and users.

Web Semantics in design delivers a cohesive structure that is pertinent to the optimization of web sites and the delivery of any form of content.

A well designed web site with well-defined structure or tree reduces continued requests when a user's browser technology is endeavouring to render your work as it is meant to be and therefore reducing the risk of a user becoming frustrated from poor authoring where they normally move on and leave a web site.

By reducing the requests called up by the user's browser rendering engine as a result of good web semantics, this will greatly aid in the delivery speed times of any web page or service being accessed by the web user or viewer, especially in the case of interactive television.

From my research, development and findings I have discovered the technology of today is now naturally branching and this has a significant relevance regarding web design and as we describe it, web semantics.

Where today web semantics as a developer is confronted with a varied set of technology computing devices such as; Tablet PC's, Laptops, Notebooks, Mobile Smart Phones, Smart TV, Readers and of course Desktop PC's.

So today in any development concerning web semantics these factors of different device types have to be seriously taken into consideration for in reality one cannot fir all and many large organizations on the web are trying to achieve this and with little success!

There is also a clear realization with search engine providers that the technology of the day does not meet, or suffice for the requirements of today's environment and there is a need now and for the future to advance human evolution through communication gateway's so users can switch platforms and services to suit their device types to successfully access and view the desired content or data sort.

So there is much to be done in the evolution of data and the way it is delivered by search engine providers. But there is also opportunity to develop new technologies and services to meet the needs of these various devices today in the way of platforms to meet demand for Desktop, Television, Smart Phones and Tablet PC's.

Looking at all of these different environments and sectors, web semantics plays a significant role in every design and structure. To enable a seamless experience for the users and one where pages, or services render almost instantly.

HTML 5.0 can offer great opportunity and where stunning creations can be achieved. As we research and develop the new benchmark standard framework of HTML 5.0, we know that with semantics first, coupled to design and then optimization, to a dedicated environment be it Desktops, Tablets, Televisions, or Smart phones for the users a successful outcome can be achieved from developing these platforms and offering greater diversity but within the confines of a structured and well authored html base of programming.

Other considerations in semantics, is to consider the variations in technology hardware devices, in relation to processing speeds, storage capacity and more.

Other considerations have to be browser interpretation and readability, along with connectivity, for be it the house next door, or an outpost in the Himalayas. The main objective first and foremost, is to ensure global reach across all borders and a cohesive and well structure design to aid in this endeavour.

Chapter Two ⊖
Web Apps Starting Faster Even Without Internet

HTML 5.0 Offline and Store for Web Apps and how they can start faster and work even when there is no internet connection.

Chapter Two: An introduction to HTML 5.0 Offline and Storage

Thanks to the HTML 5.0 App Cache, as well as the Local Storage, Indexed DB, and the File API specifications.

Off line functionality and storage today, is becoming another significant aspect again for users.

In the early, to mid-1990's, off-line storage was more related to web pages, based on the technology of the day in relation to the constraints of connectivity surrounding the world wide web where connectivity was mainly through 28 and 56k modems and as a result download speeds were very slow.

But today, HTML 5.0 brings you off line storage again with functionality for video, games eBooks and more and where reading or playing various forms of content can be stored and viewed off line.

As HTML 5.0 moves forward and with more browser software programs adopting the new RDFa framework. Greater potential and opportunity exists for a more diverse set of variant rules in content and these offerings will only increase and become available to view and participate on for a more enjoyable user experience. Be it books, films, games and music to mention a few! Where from being stored off-line you will be able to enjoy the content at a more convenient time also to you!

No longer will a news item or article be only accessible via the web. You will be able to store off-line and read later in your busy lifestyle and schedule.

The opportunities offered with HTML 5.0 for off-line storage regarding web applications and products will enable a service or program to start faster as the bulk of the content is pre stored to your devices hard drives.

As we further develop HTML 5.0 for off-line and storage content delivery especially regarding the case concerning eBooks in HTML 5.0 I am currently working on and refining. There is without doubt great synergy and opportunity for extending further services and offerings to customers and to compliment the user experience.

Chapter Three ⩊

Incredible Device Access Innovations Developed

Device Access gives you the web anywhere and at any time!

Chapter Three: An introduction to HTML 5.0 Device Access

With the new W3C benchmark core standard of HTML 5. One of the major considerations in the structured framework is to ensure successful delivery to a series of different devices namely Desk top PC's, Tablet PC's, Smart TV's, Mobile's and Smart Phones, plus now more emerging sophisticated Readers.

As developers create new HTML 5.0 services they will quickly appreciate and embrace the new framework and realize how HTML 5.0 Rocks!

More so than at any time in the history of technology devices in these past two years especially, have advanced considerably and where we have seen emerge more Tablet PC's, Smart Phones, Readers and Smart Televisions and all with the capability today to enable viewing or surfing the World Wide Web.

HTML 5.0 as a new core benchmark standard will serve to develop a framework that encapsulates these new technologies and devices. It is therefore, imperative to avoid my "Chaos Point Theory" but with this new HTML 5.0 structure where data can be delivered successfully and can be interpreted by the rendering browser engines on a device more easily these risks are greatly reduced.

HTML 5.0 offers the opportunity to develop new software solutions, but at the same time delivering a more robust framework. To ensure there is some structured order in the global world of communication, namely across the World Wide Web and where such an environment is accessed by a series of different device types.

The secret to the success of electronic media in the way of creative design is covered more in styling whereas this section covers the framework of your creations and to ensure they can be delivered successfully to these new and existing devices.

However, the first consideration is that there is a difference between each device as mentioned earlier when it comes to optimal experience for the user, whether it being a PC, Tablet, Mobile Phone, Smart TV or Reader. The latter is a device that will eventually become more connectivity based and more directly connected with the World Wide Web in the coming months and years and the HTML 5.0 standard offers the most successful delivery environment.

The fundamental considerations for successful device access for the user enjoyment experience is to be able to view and learn about your products and services with the least hindrance therefore the simplest of journey's from A to B as Steve Jobs would say!

Again success comes from keeping it simple and pure in your creative design approach.

The first thing to remember is that many mobile networks still charge for download usage or at this time there is a heated argument between mobile network providers with regards to charges and exchanging data for fee if there is a disproportionate amount from one network provider to another.

The secret and objective to all devices is to create services that are finite and highly tuned like a performance car. This relates mainly to the size of your creations and if they are too large? They will either not function correctly causing devices to hang, or leaving your viewers with a hefty bill for download charges.

The HTML 5.0 framework and core standard is exactly what it says and whilst it will offer new opportunities. It will also reign in thankfully opportunists in the community that serve to the detriment of the environment with criminality and non-productive content. Such service examples where web pages are only generated for revenue is in advertising where you visit a page that has nothing on it only advertising.

The new HTML 5.0 standards will provide for you as a developer, programmer, enthusiast, business owner, head of an Institution or Director a structure on which to build, so the new technology devices can be adopted on to the World Wide Web for data and where partners in search engine technology and security software can deliver more accurate and robust solutions in way of results that are more accurate.

There are several viewing formulas and layouts where some work better on one type of device opposed to another. But by keeping your aims focused as a developer, business, institution, authority or government on the main objectives this being the delivery of a service tailored and developed by expanding pages and serving less data on each as a consideration to the viewer so all medium devices can function successfully and this will serve you well.

The ideal solution is to develop in HTML 5.0 dedicated services as mentioned for specific devices. This is a very purist type of approach and the benefits are considerable for the development of a brand offering services and products.

However, at this time search engine partners such as Google and Yahoo will frown on your content that is regarded to be identical. For at this time the algorithms method on merit in relation to content value ranking and specifics cannot be defined at this time relating to the different devices as no distinction can be made.

However, there is a solution to this problem and something that can be overcome. But in saying that Google and other search engine providers are also making an effort to resolve these issues as they are now confronted with the problem themselves as they introduce new services covering smart tv, mobile phones and tablet devices.

Chapter Four

Greater Connectivity in Real-Time Faster Programs

Chapter 4: Efficient Connectivity means more real-time chats and faster games with HTML 5.0

Chapter Four: An introduction to HTML 5.0 Connectivity

If you are an enthusiast web master, a professional from a Government, Institution or Enterprise. Connectivity is critical for any service you publish across the World Wide Web.

Therefore from the very outset to getting your message or service out across the global community using the World Wide Web is user reach is in reality life or death.

Delivery across borders is as we all know between a series of PC's and Servers with the transfer of data packets can be a daunting prospect. The larger the packet of data it is the slower it becomes when arriving at its destination. Obviously the smaller the data packet the faster it reaches its intended viewer and user.

As Steve Job's once said, you need to think like an engineer. "I need to get from point A, to B, and by the fastest and most efficient way".

The ability to transfer your data packet from one point to another for the recipient is not that straight forward as a number of factors come into play.

This relates to the actual hardware devices releasing and receiving the data, the "trunking" or "pipes" with regards to the telecommunications networks that are to be used and also regarding design structure of your electronic media data.

Other important factors come from within the recipient's hardware device namely browser, operating system and processing speeds of the PC or Mobile Device.

You also have to consider the device type receiving the data as mentioned for with the emergence of smart phone technology today and tablet PC's, plus Smart TV. The device receiving the data may not necessarily be a PC on a desk at home or at work.

There are also other elements regarding transportation of data packets. This obviously relates to traffic and where in most instances devices from point A to B will derive at the fastest route for delivery but as a result different networks and services will have a considerable bearing in relation to delivery and speed.

The new HTML 5.0 fifth core element benchmark standard will help provide a more resilient and speedier solution for Governments, Institutions, Enterprises, Enthusiasts and most importantly the user.

One of the foremost objectives is to create a global communications structure with a sense of order from the framework you are developing.

Today as you know even when searching for information you can find yourself on a web page that bears no relevance to the subject matter you are seeking.

The introduction of a rigid HTML 5.0 core language will help users and network providers and most importantly search engines and browser software technology for the programming underway today by all parties will be able to determine relevance, accessibility, semantics and speed for connectivity delivery with the new HTML 5.0 framework.

Chapter Five 🎬

Audio and Video Now at the Forefront of HTML 5.0

Audio and video are first class citizens in the HTML 5.0 web today and living in harmony with your apps and sites. Lights, camera, action!

Chapter Five: An introduction to HTML 5.0 Multimedia

Multimedia is a very powerful platform and environment for getting your message across for the sale or promotion of any products or services.

HTML 5.0 provides a powerful benchmark standard to let this happen and across a series of devices and technologies today that we have come to know.

19

Even browser technology today as programming continues will significantly advance multimedia from the HTML 5.0 framework and now unleashing tremendous opportunity.

With the emergence today of Interactive Television, Tablet touch technology and mobile smart phone devices the new HTML 5.0 RDFa framework will aid and bolster these ideas and ambitions for greater multimedia creativity.

They say a picture can say a 1,000 words, well multimedia streaming and broadcasting can deliver atmosphere and inspire the user imagination.

The continued advancement of gaming and multimedia on the World Wide Web as a commercial viability in relation to films, music and more will see such services further advanced from HTML 5.0

On demand interactive services are here to stay and when as a partner with Microsoft on the Web TV project back in the late 1990's I always believed eventually the interactive television will be the homing technology of the future based on the usage and demand where most if not all of family household devote time through such an entertainment platform.

In the coming weeks and months more features and promoting will be more than noticeable regarding Smart TV and the interactive set top box more like a computer today will no doubt be taking another quantum leap soon so smart tv services are reachable to every household and the HTML 5.0 framework will help by providing the vehicle for this to be achieved.

Chapter Six

Greater Stunning Visual Effects
Browser Rendering

Stunning 3D and High Definition visual effects can now be successfully delivered by the new HTML 5.0 framework.

Chapter Six: An introduction to 3D and Visual Effects with HTML 5.0

The World Wide Web has come a long way since its very early commercial days and where Eric Bina achieved the impossible as it seemed at then at the National Centre for Super Computing at Champagne, in Illinois back in the early 1990's with close friend Marc Andreessen. When they began a journey with colleagues on the regarding the commercial World Wide Web as we know it today, where from successful programming they were able to introduce images into a browser program software known

21

as Mosaic.

Those very early days only saw 16 colour formats of imagery whereas today, we discuss 32 million pixels as a matter of the norm.

With the advancements today in communication especially telecommunications and with the advancing of broad band we are able to now deliver more dynamic rich media content.

As a result, 3D special effects will only come to the fore more as we see and enjoy films downloaded and streamed today.

This is a far cry from the early interactive WebTV days that I worked on and first began to develop on the Microsoft Partner Program in the early and mid-1990's where we had to develop and work with 28k modem connections and only up to 5 to 10 megabyte set top storage boxes.

Today's set top boxes and smart televisions are grand designs of computing and as a result delivering an interactive web experience for many.

Visual impact has been a key factor as mentioned earlier to any web design and since the web's early beginnings 3D special effects are again at the very forefront today!

The technology advancements over past years has been restricted not from the programming and ability to create stunning imagery but the framework or the environment to deliver such content. Well, not any longer, for HTML 5.0 does just that and faster and with a more resilient framework environment that benefits all, including browser software, operating systems and lastly, but most importantly for the user.

HTML 5.0 unlocks the World of 3D Special Effects and Visual High Definition Art or Photography.

With HTML 5.0 the new standard allows for further creativity in 3D special effects, but again with a consideration to implement standards to ensure an orderly structure.

Digital photography is also again today a winner as advancements continue at breakneck speed and where every smart phone has a built in camera as one example and the technology today can now benefit all with the new HTML 5.0 framework to deliver your stunning images across the web or to send to loved ones the other side of the planet.

The winners in this new competitive era of global communications winning the day will be these very visual dynamic effects and you the user.

HTML 5.0 enables you to deliver bolder visual images to capture your audience imagination and desire for a product or service in a commercial sense and faster as technology browser rendering also advances and evolves with the new standard.

Developing new web sites and services in HTML 5.0 will enable you to bring your web sites alive!

Always remember human nature behaviour and the power of what the eye can see!

Images are invariably one of the main decision making points in relation to buying products.

In fact the statistics are; 35% brand, 60% visual impact and 5% product information and after sales service.

Always remember in most instances with reference to web sites photographs and visual images such features can be so often an after-thought and the last consideration.

Visual imagery is a key essential aid and should be at the very forefront of your mind, when mapping out a new service for your users if you are an enterprise reader.

Chapter Seven ✿
Web Apps Integration Providing Faster Web Content

Making you web apps faster and more dynamic web content using the new benchmark standard of HTML 5.0

Chapter Seven: An introduction to Performance with HTML 5.0

Make your Web Apps and dynamic web content faster with a variety of techniques and technologies.

Such as Web Workers and XML Http Request 2. No user should ever wait on your watch.

Some parts of performance from HTML 5.0 we have already mentioned and aligned to 'Semantics' and in many respects the structure of a creation and has a significant relevance for the successful delivery of data for the user and if the creative design is concise it will assist in a faster delivery of content, programs and services.

When a user connects to a web site's data on a server the browser calls up delivery requests of the data and images on those specific pages and so by reducing the number of delivery requests via a user's browser ensures a faster and more seamless experience for the user and not having to wait around.

In my Research and Development of HTML 5.0 I understand how there can be contradictions abound in the development of any service using technology.

One of the biggest problem areas again relates to criteria's of scoring or the importance and relevance with the results in search engines.

If a search engine determines your web site as a result of more written content scores higher than say a web site's creatively designed and with mainly images it can often be to the detriment of the product, brand or service being offered.

To combine the both or in fact whatever you add to a web page increases the packet size of the web page and with the higher chance that such a page with more content will perform slower.

Today's user wants instant content. We have become a society for action and information now and so any delay of large web page content can be a permanent negative and can be said as "its history" and the user will no longer wait but move on.

As like in life and it is a very challenging proposition here. Where you have to design a home page that scores high for content and loads almost instantly there is a need for compromise, however this should not be the case but sadly it is today, but HTML 5.0 will address this injustice that has existed since the commercial World Wide Web's beginning.

With the new framework of HTML 5.0 this new technology framework will greatly help you achieve greater performance, speed and efficiency for a more enjoyable and dynamic user experience. This will be achieved through design for better performance of your web site and then go hand in hand with the new browser technology advancements now adopting the new framework of HTML 5.0

I suppose the current dilemma we have and a good analogy is; it is like designing a Formula One Car that can travel at 260 mph, but expected to perform on a road network only suitable for horse and cart with a 30 mph speed limit restriction.

HTML 5.0 thankfully is now being seriously adopted by major browser developers. Apple are very far ahead with HTML 5.0 as are Mozilla Firefox (Netscape) and now introducing more dynamic features such as the Apple Safari HTML 5.0 reader technology to the Safari Browser rendering engine and where recently Mozilla had completely scrapped their previous updated browser versions and now introduced the most latest and advanced browser with noticeable performance difference to previous versions and so delivering a new era of browser technology for the user deriving from the HTML 5.0 framework.

The HTML 5.0 new RDFa environment provides far greater performance and opens up many opportunities to deliver faster services and more sophisticated content. However, as already mentioned design in the way of semantics has a significant bearing now and especially with validation of web sites and web pages.

These standards whilst not seen in the search engine optimization data results do have a significant relevance in relation to performance scoring and are of critical importance between browser and web site.

HTML 5.0 is high octane and from development of web pages

with over a megabyte of data are rendering now in less than 2 seconds and when you consider the average web page in size is around 25 to 95 kb, this is a quantum leap.

I have also conducted tests on many web pages and have found even web pages being three times the size of Google's the performance own web pages the results have produced pages to be faster. The figures may even be more rapid and dynamic in the near future for at this time many tests are based on technologies developed within the HTML 4.01 framework in comparison to the new benchmark standard of HTML 5.0.

To aid and help in optimization and performance derived from my research and development. I have published in the last chapter useful reference sites and resources to direct you to more detailed information on HTML 5.0 for authoring understanding and testing.

Also another one of my new developments that can be successful with HTML 5.0 is regarding the creation of **'Runways'** to help maintain a high scoring value for content as currently required by search engines but also bringing dynamic visual appeal!

Runway is a way to deliver a large amount of content desired on a home page that can be distributed across several pages reducing packet size so the landing home pages load much faster but at the same time retaining essential data across two to three key pages all immediately linked with the landing home page. This concept can be invaluable and a method worth considering when posed with such a dilemma.

Chapter Eight ∃
Greater Stylization Using Cascading Style Sheets

CSS 3.0 delivers a wide range of stylization effects for more dynamic web content in HTML 5.0

Chapter Eight: An introduction to Styling with HTML 5.0

Creative design is critical to the successful delivery of your message to the masses. By working as a developer, programmer or enthusiast and applying these new core benchmark standards. The results will be significant and you will also become a friend to providers in the industry for delivering a cohesive and structured electronic media.

HTML 5.0 Best Practices in Creative Styling for the Structure of your Work as an Insight

I am sure we have all seen many advertisements for "Building Your Own Web Sites" or "Get a Web Site in 5 Minutes", but reality is and has always been the case. As like any trades or crafts computer sciences comes as a title with the words frustration, tears, emotion, confusion and the need for more answers to mention a few!

The fact of the matter is creative styling and design that encapsulates programming is an art and a science in its self. There are very few professions that have a great many dynamics to consider on the drawing board.

It is true that a successful web site design comes only from dedication and knowledge to technical authoring and the ability to architecturally map out an electronic medium service that needs to be published internationally and viewed by a few or in the millions.

Successful styling as in life comes from the word objective! This invariably relates to the retaining of brand identity the services and products being offered.

Visual presentation is just as important as content. But just as importantly is the successful delivery of the electronic publication.

The most common mistakes in design is to add regardless of thought new technologies, programs and features and not thinking of the user and his or her device accessing the data.

This may well demonstrate a web designer's accruement but may serve to the detriment of the brand if customers are unable to access the services web site.
You could have a web site all singing, bells and whistles created from your new monster workstation. But in reality think 'Kiss' and

remain focused on the objective at hand and that is developing awareness of the brand and selling the services or products.

To achieve this think like an engineer as mentioned before getting from A to B and the recipient being able to view the electronic published material successfully so they can become informed of the brand, service, or products.

Some of the most successful marketing campaigns of the past have derived from just presenting a brand marquee. This can still be very often the case today and seen in conventional magazine publishing.

Continuity is also critical for the viewing user if familiar with a brand they would not expect to see something entirely different or quirky.

You also have to consider the very many different hardware devices and software programs such as operating systems, browser programs and the hardware capability of the user's device viewing your electronic media.

You also need to consider your viewer base from novice to proficient so you are spanning all ages. Your creation has to therefore endeavour to accommodate all.

To be able to achieve this successfully and to attain and retain customers and followers rather than loose them is to focus on the brand, products, or services.

Design styling, can be creative and imaginative, but also structured. You will not be thanked by the viewer, if their PC hangs, or the browser crashes, or they cannot navigate.

One frustrating example often seen is when you go to a navigation point on a web page with a drop down menu and before the user can click on the link it disappears and then takes you to the wrong page.

Creative Web Designers can be part of a problem regarding the successful delivery of a brand, product or service. But by applying a more puritanical approach, the experience for the user can be seamless, gets the brand across to the masses and therefore introduces products and services successfully.

The myth regarding building a web site in five minutes or on your own without any skills will only spell disaster and this is a polite warning to any!

There are many factors in creative design and styling that includes search engine optimization to mention just one.

If a search engine is unable to index a web site due to timing out because of poor design. You can have the best product in the World but if no one will ever know about it the exercise does not only become costly but academic!

Clients and customers will appreciate honesty and objectives, for a structured design and one that is successful. As a developer your reputation only stands on delivery of successful services.

To create excellent design and efficiency HTM 5.0 encourages you to develop CSS (Cascading Style Sheets) 3.0 where you can code and programme design that can be with universally applied to all web pages creating continuity.

By using cascading style sheets in styling you can determine fonts, size, images, backgrounds and more from just one or two document pages and the code applying to tens if not hundreds of web pages.

Once such a program document is called up the bulk of the web design is then delivered to your user so every web page with content variations will load faster creating a seamless and enjoyable experience for the user.

Chapter Eight: CSS 3.0 Validation of HTML 5.0

Finally, to take a tour of HTML 5.0 in action I have set up the following web site address: www.alastairagutter.com/html5/

All the photographs in this book are from this working web site.

Chapter Nine
Useful References and Resources for Developers

Please find here below valuable links to further explore and acquire further knowledge of the new benchmark standard and framework HTML 5.0 for the World Wide Web.

Chapter Nine: HTML 5.0 for a Faster High Octane Performance for Users

1/. Quality Assurance Web Semantics Structure Extractor
URL: http://www.w3.org/2003/12/semantic-extractor.html

2/. HTML 5.0 World Wide Web Consortium Validator
URL: http://validator.w3.org/

3/. CSS 3.0 World Wide Web Consortium Validator
URL: http://jigsaw.w3.org/css-validator/

4/. W3C Working Progress Framework of HTML 5.0
URL: http://www.w3.org/TR/html5/

5/. W3C HTML 5.0 Master Draft of Framework Structure
URL: http://www.w3.org/html/wg/drafts/html/master/

6/. HTML 5 Live Design Simplicity Created by Alastair Agutter
URL: http://www.alastairagutter.com/html5/

7/. W3 Schools for Tutorials and Coding on HTML 5.0
URL: http://www.w3schools.com/html/html5_intro.asp
8/. Wikipedia HTML 5.0 Dictionary Document
URL: http://en.wikipedia.org/wiki/HTML5

9/. W3C HTML 5.0 Logo, Stickers and Promotion Resources
URL: http://www.w3.org/html/logo/

10/. Getting Inside Google's Head Book - Optimization
URL: http://www.alastairagutter.com/books/getting-inside-googles-head-book.html

Chapter Ten
About the Author and Related Publications

Alastair R Agutter was born in Farnborough, England in 1958 to English parents. He is a freelance (self-employed) Writer, Philosopher, Logistician, Theoretical Physicist, Author, Publisher, Naturalist, Environmentalist, Computer Scientist, Creative Digital Artist and Proud Father of Five Children.

Chapter Ten: The Five Minute Guide to HTML 5.0 Book

His most recent book for technology has been "Getting Inside Google's Head" for web site optimization and has been an Amazon Best Seller and the book is an essential reference to achieving the best in web site performance and search engine rankings by taking the reader through the 13 key essential elements.

"Getting Inside Google's Head Book" is available as a printed paperback or digital publication.

Alastair is a passionate advocate for the environment and a naturalist at heart, with a great respect for all living creatures and with founding principles for the preservation of all species, many sadly under threat today from climate change.

He believes there is no reason why the human race cannot learn from quantum mechanics, and co-exist with the environment and all living species on Earth.

To find out more, about the author's, new up and coming book releases, and to get the latest news please visit

www.alastairagutter.com

Author Acknowledgements:

A current Member of Microsoft Partner Research Panel.

Noted in Phillips: - Who's Who Directory 2001

Acknowledged in 1999:- by Hudson Institute, for Advancing Computer Science Internationally.

Acknowledged in 2008:- by the American Autobiographical Society for the advancement of Computer Sciences to Humanity.

A Former Partner Member of Microsoft WebTV

A Former Founding Member of Netscape DevEdge Team UK

A Former Member of the BBC Backstage

A Current Google Program Partner

An Amazon Associate Partner

Author's Web Site: www.alastairagutter.com

THE FIVE MINUTE GUIDE TO HTML 5.0

The New Fifth Core Element Architecture of the World Wide Web

By Alastair R Agutter

www.alastairagutter.com

PUBLISHED ON

First Published: 23rd May 2014

PUBLISHED AND PRINTED BY

Create Space Independent Publishing an Amazon Group Member

Paperback Edition for International Distribution

ISBN-10: 1499661037

ISBN-13: 978-1499661033

Getting Inside Google's Head

Title

Servers

RSS

Graphics

Content

Feeds

Google

The Key Elements To Web Site Optimization Success!

"Full Colour Collectors Edition"

Domain

Rich Media

Social Networks

Hosting

Keywords

Description

Grammar

Written by Alastair R Agutter

www.ingramcontent.com/pod-product-compliance
Lightning Source LLC
Chambersburg PA
CBHW041147050326
40689CB00001B/519